The Near Planets

DONNA BAILEY

RSVP

RAINTREE
STECK-VAUGHN
PUBLISHERS
The Steck-Vaughn Company
Austin, Texas

How to Use This Book

This book tells you many things about the planets nearest the Sun. There is a Table of Contents on the next page. It shows you what each double page of the book is about. For example, pages 8 and 9 tell you about ''Mercury: Next to the Sun.''

On many of these pages you will find words that are printed in **bold** type. The bold type shows you that these words are in the Glossary on pages 46 and 47. The Glossary explains the meaning of those words that may be new to you.

At the very end of the book there is an Index. The Index tells you where to find certain words in the book. For example, you can use it to look up words like space probes, Solar System, asteroids, and may other words to do with the near planets.

Trade Edition published 1992 © Steck-Vaughn Company

Library of Congress Cataloging-in-Publication Data

Bailey, Donna.
   The near planets / written by Donna Bailey.
     p.   cm.—(Facts about)
   Includes index.
   Summary: Examines the four planets that lie closest to the sun, discussing their composition, movements, and moons.
    ISBN 0-8114-2523-1 Hardcover Library Binding
    ISBN 0-8114-5201-8 Softcover Binding
   1. Planets—Juvenile literature. [1. Planets.] I. Title. II. Series: Facts about (Austin, Tex.)
QB602.B34 1991   90-40078
523.4—dc20   CIP AC
Printed and bound in the United States of America
   3 4 5 6 7 8 9 0 LB 95 94 93

Contents

Introduction

The world we live on is a **planet** called Earth. The Earth is one of nine planets that travel around the Sun. Each trip that Earth makes is a year long.

The planets Mercury, Venus, Earth, and Mars are the nearest to the Sun so they are sometimes called the inner planets. Jupiter, Saturn, Uranus, Neptune, and Pluto are the outer planets.

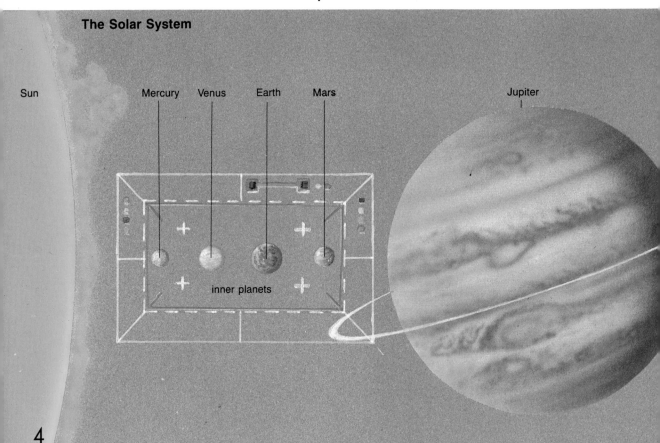

The Solar System

Sun   Mercury   Venus   Earth   Mars   Jupiter

inner planets

The two planets nearest to the Sun are baking hot. The farthest planets from the Sun are bitterly cold.

From Earth the planets look like stars. In the photograph the planet Venus is shining brightly below the Moon. As Venus travels around the Sun it comes near to Earth so we can see it clearly.

The Sun and the planets with their **moons** make up the **Solar System**.

Saturn

Uranus

Neptune

Pluto

outer planets

The Truth about Space

When we look at the night sky, we can see five stars which seem to be moving. All the other stars stay in the same place. These five moving points of light are planets.

Long ago people thought that gods and goddesses lived on the planets so they named the planets after them.

The planet Mars which has a reddish glow is named after the Roman god of war. People thought that Mars could make wars on Earth.

a space story about robots from Venus

Many people read stories about space travel and landing on other planets.

Astronomers want to know what it is really like in space. They use huge **telescopes** to look at the stars and planets.

By 1986 most of the planets in the Solar System had been visited by **space probes**. The picture shows a Venera probe sent by the Soviet Union in 1975 to explore Venus.

Mercury: Next to the Sun

Mercury is the planet nearest the Sun. Never try to look at Mercury through a telescope yourself as the Sun's rays may damage your eyes.

In 1965 radio signals were sent to Mercury from the huge **radio telescope** on Puerto Rico in the Caribbean. The information bounced back by the signals told us how Mercury spins.

The picture shows a photograph taken by the space Mariner 10 in 1974 and 1975. Mercury's **surface** is a rocky desert so hot nothing can live on it.

the world's largest radio telescope on Puerto Rico is set up in a valley

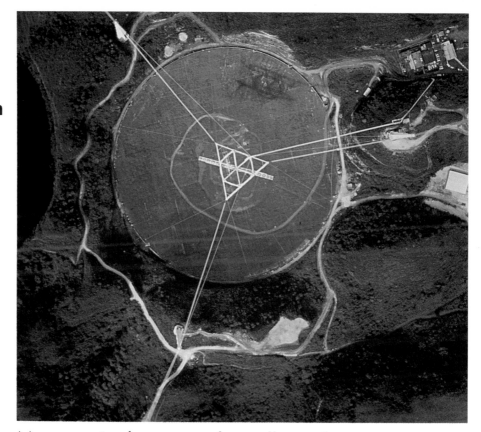

Mercury is the second smallest planet in the Solar System. It is less than half the size of Earth.

Facts about Mercury

Diameter	3,100 mi
Mass	$\frac{1}{16}$ of Earth
Distance from the Sun	36 million mi
Period of rotation	59 days
Period of revolution	88 days
Tilt of axis	0°
Gravity on the surface	$\frac{2}{5}$ of Earth
Average temperature	660°F (day)
	−275°F (night)
Atmosphere	almost none

Earth   Mercury

Mercury: Flying Past the Planet

The picture shows the space probe Mariner 10 passing the rim of Mercury. After the probe left Earth, it traveled past Venus and Mercury and then swung around to **orbit** the Sun. The photos from Mariner 10 showed that there are mountains and **plains** on Mercury's surface. Mercury is covered with **craters** and it also has deep cracks in its surface which were made when it was first formed.

The **core** of Mercury is very hot. It contains **molten** iron. The core is covered by a thick layer of rock called the **mantle**.

Mercury has no air and no life on it. There is no **atmosphere** to block out the Sun's rays.
During the day the heat of the Sun scorches the rocky surface, but at night it gets freezing cold.

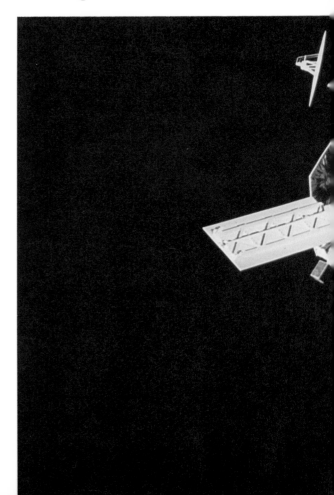

the core of Mercury is slowly cooling and shrinking

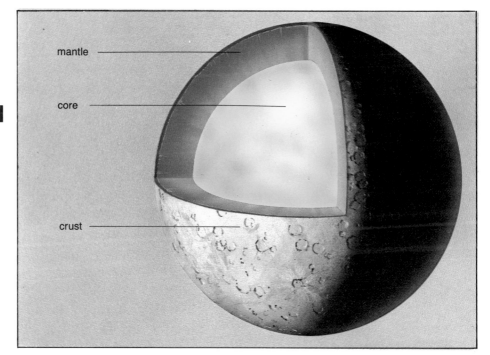

mantle

core

crust

Venus: The Nearest Planet to Earth

The picture shows one of the photographs of Venus taken in 1974 by Mariner 10. The photographs showed that the planet is covered in thick clouds. The clouds **reflect** the sunlight and make Venus easy to see from Earth.

Facts about Venus	
Diameter	7,500 mi
Mass	4/5 of Earth
Distance from the Sun	67 million mi
Period of rotation	243 days
Period of revolution	225 days
Tilt of axis	2°
Gravity on the surface	4/5 of Earth
Average temperature	870°F
Atmosphere	carbon dioxide

Earth   Venus

Radio signals bounced back from Venus
show that the planet turns very slowly.
It is the only planet to spin backward.

You can look at Venus through
binoculars or a small telescope.
You will see a **crescent** that changes
shape as Venus moves around the Sun.
From Earth we can only see the half of
Venus that is lit up by the Sun.

**the orbit
of Venus
passes
close to
the Earth**

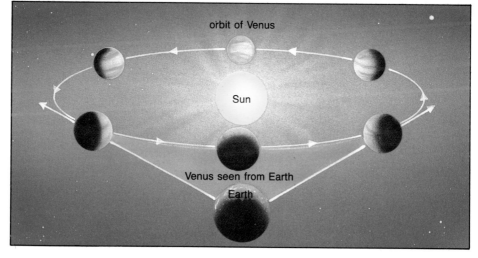

orbit of Venus

Sun

Venus seen from Earth

Earth

Venus: An Orange Sky

The surface of Venus is mostly flat.
It is covered with stones, boulders, and
lava thrown out from **volcanoes**.

The yellow clouds on Venus float in
an atmosphere of **carbon dioxide** gas.
The carbon dioxide gas presses down on
the surface of Venus with a force
90 times as great as the pressure of
air on Earth. The clouds on Venus are
made of tiny drops of **sulfuric acid**.
The clouds trap the Sun's heat and
make the surface of Venus very hot.
So hot lead and tin would melt.

It is even hotter on Venus than on
Mercury and there is no water.
No life can exist in such a place.
   The large core inside Venus is made
of iron, nickel, and other metals.
The solid crust floats on a mantle of
rocks.

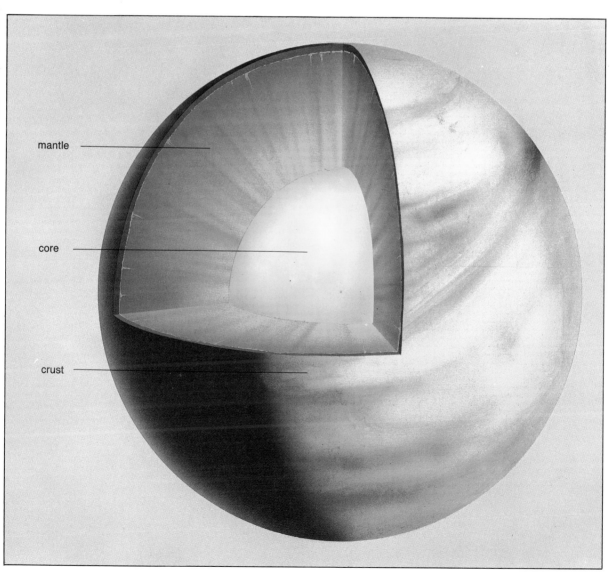

mantle

core

crust

Venus: Probes and Maps

In 1978 the United States sent Pioneer Venus I to make a map of Venus. The probe did not land but went into orbit around Venus for many months. It took many photographs of the planet's surface. These show that most of Venus is a smooth plain.

In this photograph the low plains have been colored blue. The higher areas of Aphrodite Land and Ishtar Land have been colored green and yellow. The highest land, the Maxwell Mountains, is colored brown and red. These mountains are higher than Earth's Mount Everest.

Pioneer Venus 1 took photographs of Venus

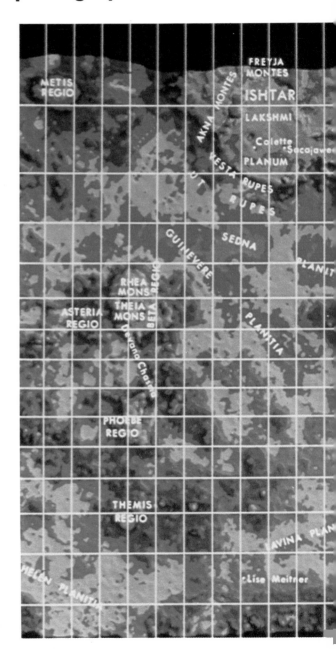

The Soviets have sent many probes to Venus.
Some were crushed before they landed.
In 1975 two probes landed but stopped
working after an hour, perhaps because
of the acid in the air above Venus.

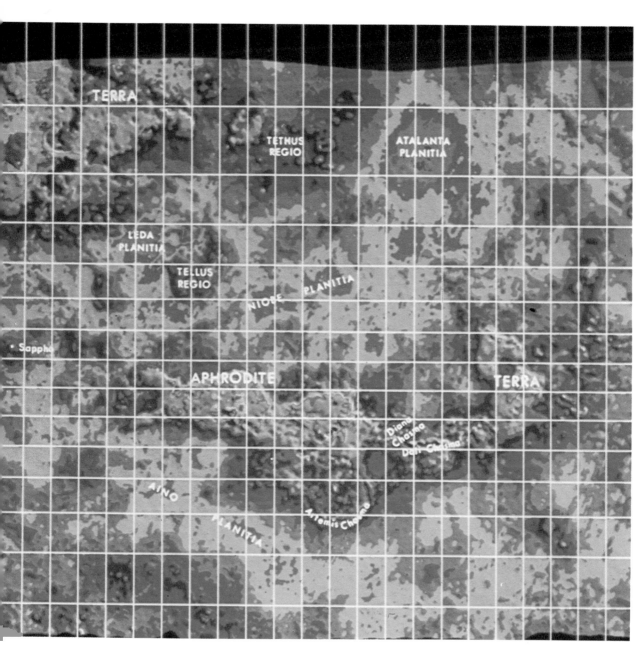

Earth: Our Home

The photograph shows Earth as it is seen from space. You can see the ice and snow of Antarctica to the south, and the forests and deserts of Africa to the north. The blue areas are the South Atlantic Ocean and the Indian Ocean. Swirls of white clouds surround Earth.

The way Earth spins is very important to us. It gives us day and night. It is day in the half of the Earth facing the Sun. In the other half, which is in shadow, it is night.

The Earth's **axis** is tilted. This makes the weather change and gives us the different **seasons**. When it is autumn in North America, the northern part of the Earth is tilting away from the Sun and so the days get colder.

Facts about the Earth	
Diameter	7,926.41 mi
Mass	6 sextillion, 588 quintillion tons
Distance from the Sun	93 million mi
Period of rotation	23 hours 56 minutes
Period of revolution	365 days 6 hours
Tilt of axis	23.4°
Average temperature	70°F
Atmosphere	mainly nitrogen and oxygen
Number of moons	1

Earth: Inside Our Planet

The Earth's core is a solid ball of iron. Around it is a very hot layer of molten iron which is surrounded by a heavy mantle of rocks. The Earth's surface or crust is made up of **plates**.

The heat from inside the Earth makes these plates move slowly over the crust. In some places the plates bump into each other and rocks in the crust fold up to make mountains such as the Andes or the Himalayas. At other places the plates slide past each other or move apart. **Earthquakes** happen at the edges of plates when rocks slide over each other.

The movement of the plates causes holes to appear in the Earth's crust. In these places there are many volcanoes.

The photograph shows a volcano on Hawaii. A river of red-hot lava bubbles up from inside the Earth and flows down the mountainside.

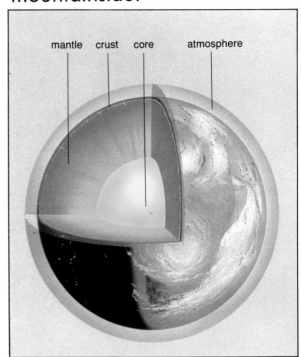

mantle   crust   core   atmosphere

Earth: The Air Around Us

The Earth's atmosphere is made up of
air, which is a mixture of gases.
Nearly four-fifths of the air is
nitrogen and the rest is **oxygen**.
The air also contains **water vapor**.
All living things need oxygen, water,
and sunlight to stay alive. Earth is
the only planet with oxygen. It is the
only planet that has many different
kinds of plants and animals.

If a rock from space enters the atmosphere, it slows down and is burned up. A **Space Shuttle** must be fitted with special tiles to protect it so that it will not burn up when it comes back from space.

The northern lights are made by tiny **particles** from the Sun striking the gases in the atmosphere and making patterns of color.

the northern lights

Earth: Out into Space

Landsat

The computer photograph shows lower Cape Cod, Massachusetts. It was taken by a Landsat **satellite**. Landsat pictures are colored to show up towns and plant life and other things of interest to scientists.

The satellites are launched into space by a **rocket** or put in orbit by riding on the back of a Space Shuttle. Five of these Landsat satellites were launched between 1972 and 1984.

Scientists use satellite photographs to make weather forecasts, or to help find out where to mine oil, coal, or metals. Some satellites can carry television programs and telephone calls.

Very strong beams of light can be sent from Earth by machines called **lasers** to a satellite in space. The satellite bounces the beam back to Earth and scientists then time the beam from different parts of the Earth. The scientists can then measure the movements of the Earth's crust.

The Moon: Our Partner

The Moon circles around our Earth, and both of them go around the Sun together. Many other planets have moons going around them, too.

The Moon reflects light from the Sun. From Earth, we see different amounts of light and shadow on the Moon. This makes the Moon seem to change its shape during the course of a month from new moon to full moon and back.

During an **eclipse** of the Moon, the Earth blocks off the light from the Sun. The Moon disappears in the Earth's shadow. This happens two or three times a year.

Facts about the Moon	
Diameter	2,160 mi
Mass	1/81 of the Earth
Distance from the Earth	238,857 mi
Period of rotation	27 days 8 hours
Period of revolution	27 days 8 hours
Tilt of axis	1.5°
Gravity on the surface	1/6 of the Earth
Temperature	230°F (day) −290°F (night)
Atmosphere	none

Earth   Moon

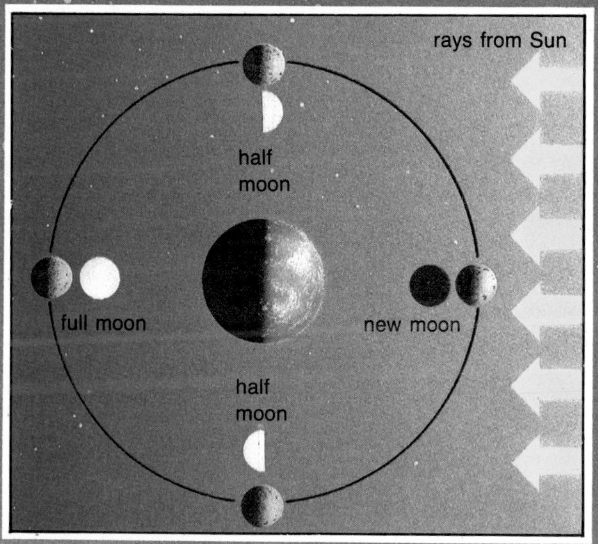

rays from Sun

half
moon

full moon

new moon

half
moon

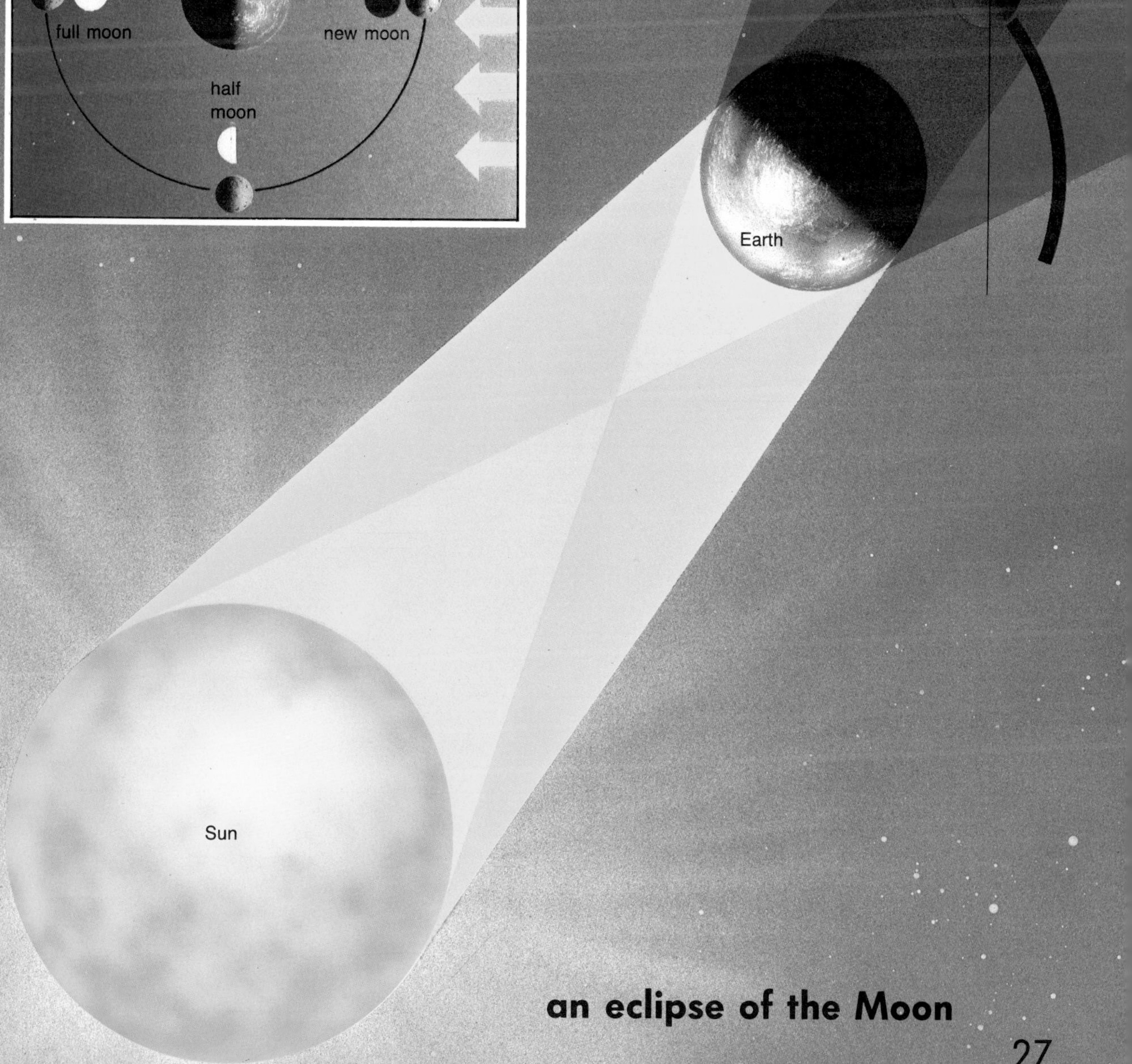

Earth's shadow

Moon's orbit

Earth

Sun

an eclipse of the Moon

The Moon: Bare Rock

The surface of the Moon is made of rock
and is covered with **dust** and craters.
There are big craters with high walls
which form the Moon's mountains.
There are also large plains that
astronomers long ago thought were
covered with water, so they gave them
the names of seas and oceans.
Today we know that the plains are dry.

The picture shows the Earth rising
above the rim of the Moon.

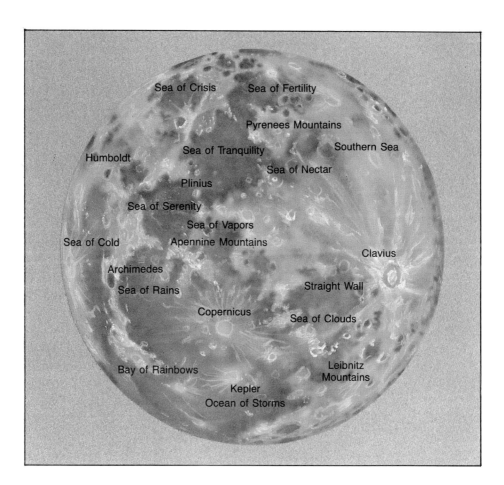

Sea of Crisis Sea of Fertility

Pyrenees Mountains

Sea of Tranquility Southern Sea

Humboldt Sea of Nectar

Plinius

Sea of Serenity

Sea of Vapors

Sea of Cold Apennine Mountains Clavius

Archimedes

Sea of Rains Straight Wall

Copernicus Sea of Clouds

Bay of Rainbows Leibnitz Mountains

Kepler
Ocean of Storms

The map shows the side of the Moon that we can see from Earth. It shows some of the Moon's many craters. The largest crater, called Clavius, is 143 miles wide.

The Moon, like the Earth, has a crust, mantle, and core, but the Moon's crust does not move.

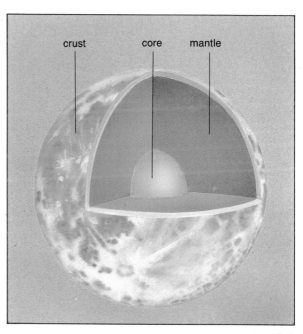

crust core mantle

The Moon: Touchdown

For centuries people wanted to go to the Moon.

In 1966 a Soviet space probe called Luna 9 landed on the Moon and sent back the first photograph of its surface. This showed an empty planet covered with rocks.

The big picture shows the giant Saturn V rocket which was launched in 1969. The rocket lifted the Apollo 11 spacecraft out of the Earth's atmosphere. On July 20, two American astronauts were the first humans to land on the Moon. They landed from a **lunar module**, while the main part of the spacecraft stayed in orbit around the Moon.

Neil Armstrong and Edwin Aldrin stayed on the surface of the Moon for 2 ½ hours. Later there were five more Apollo flights and landings on its surface.

For three of the landings the astronauts used a special Moon car to drive around and collect soil and pieces of rock.

the astronauts collected
over 830 pounds of rock
from the Moon

USA

Mars: The Red Planet

Mars is the fourth planet from the Sun and it shines like a big red star. At its **north pole** there is a white ice cap throughout the year, just as on Earth. This cap is made up of the gas carbon dioxide. It is so cold at the **south pole** that the gas freezes. It becomes solid and white and falls like snow.

Mars is tilted on its axis so it has seasons, too.

During autumn and winter the white caps grow very big as more gas freezes. In spring and summer each cap gets smaller.

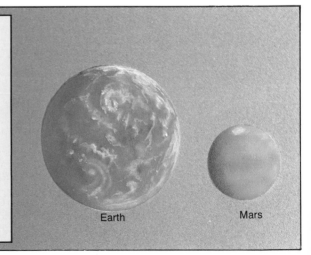

Facts about Mars

Diameter:	4,200 mi
Mass:	1/10 of the Earth
Distance from the Sun:	141 million mi
Period of rotation:	24 hours, 37 minutes
Period of revolution:	687 days
Tilt of axis:	24°
Gravity on the surface:	2/5 of the Earth
Average temperature:	−9°F
Atmosphere:	carbon dioxide
Number of moons:	2

Earth   Mars

we can see
the frozen
gas around
the south
pole of Mars
and an area
of volcanoes
to the north

Mars: Craters and Volcanoes

Astronomers think that Mars has a thick crust and a small core. The crust is made up of rocks that contain iron.

The space probe Viking I took this photograph. It shows the planet Mars, covered with red rocks. That is why Mars looks red from out in space.

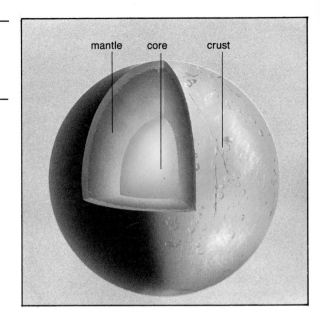

mantle   core   crust

Mars has deep valleys made by movements in the planet's crust, and it has many deep craters.

There are also mountains made of huge piles of lava.

The photograph, taken by one of the Viking probes, shows one of the huge volcanoes on Mars. The volcanoes are no longer pouring out lava, but they may erupt again one day.

Among the rocks on Mars are banks of red sand **dunes**. Sometimes there are huge dust storms that hide the surface of the planet. The dust storms make different patterns of sand markings on the surface of Mars.

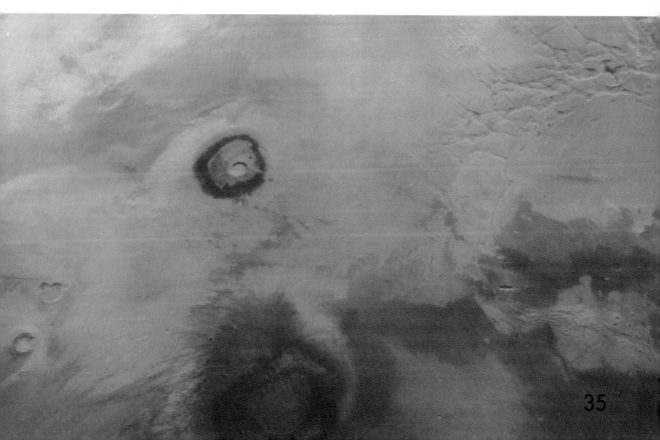

Mars: In Search of Life

When people on Earth saw icy caps on Mars they thought there must be water on the planet. They thought there might be life there.

In 1965 the United States sent the first probe, called Mariner 4, to fly past Mars. This was followed by Mariners 6 and 7 which took photographs showing craters on the surface.

In 1971 Mariner 9 went into orbit around Mars and sent back photographs of the whole surface. These showed big **canyons** and volcanoes on Mars.

The Viking probes carried television cameras and an arm for collecting soil.

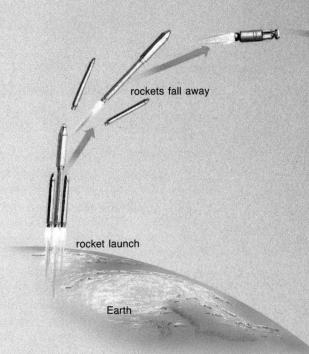

rockets fall away

rocket launch

Earth

The Viking probes were shot into space by rockets. The probes took 10 months to reach Mars, where they divided into two sections. A lander section flew down to the surface of Mars. The main section of the probe went into orbit around the planet.

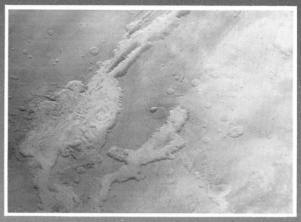

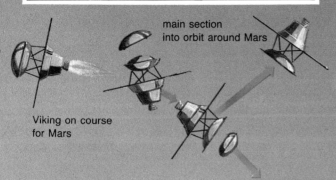

Viking on course
for Mars

main section
into orbit around Mars

this photograph of Mars
shows the deep canyons
which stretch across the
surface of the planet

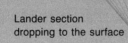

Lander section
dropping to the surface

the Viking landers
measured the temperature
and speed of the winds
and did other tests

Mars

The Moons of Mars

As Mars travels around the Sun it is circled by two moons, called Phobos and Deimos. These tiny moons orbit Mars in a counter-clockwise direction. They look like flying potatoes. Phobos may break up one day.

orbit of Mars

**the surface
of Phobos**

Phobos and Deimos are dark lumps of
rock which are dotted with craters.
Phobos also has deep channels that may
be cracks in its surface.

The photograph shows the deep craters
and scars on Phobos where other rocks
have crashed into it.

39

Mini-planets

In between Mars and Jupiter, the first of the outer planets, are many tiny planets called **asteroids**. They are very small compared with the size of our Moon.

Astronomers keep track of about 3,000 asteroids, but there are countless others that are too small to record.

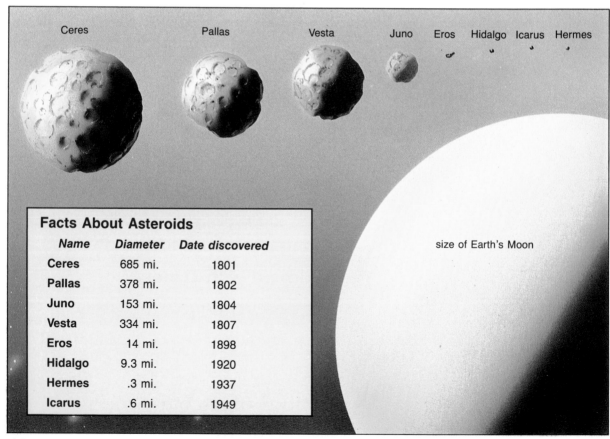

Ceres   Pallas   Vesta   Juno   Eros   Hidalgo   Icarus   Hermes

size of Earth's Moon

Facts About Asteroids

Name	Diameter	Date discovered
Ceres	685 mi.	1801
Pallas	378 mi.	1802
Juno	153 mi.	1804
Vesta	334 mi.	1807
Eros	14 mi.	1898
Hidalgo	9.3 mi.	1920
Hermes	.3 mi.	1937
Icarus	.6 mi.	1949

Most asteroids are found in an **asteroid belt** that divides the inner planets from the outer planets. Asteroids move around the Sun just like the bigger planets. They make very long journeys through the Solar System. Some asteroids have orbits that take them outside the asteroid belt and quite close to some of the planets.

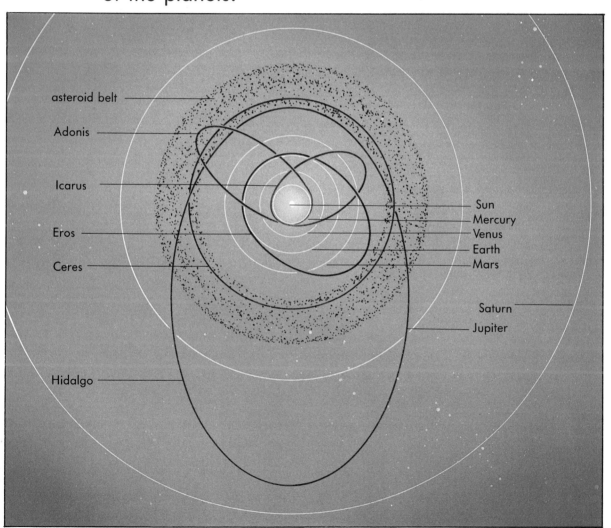

Space Rocks

Thousands of tiny bits of rock and metal strike Earth from space every day. These pieces are called **meteoroids**. As they enter the Earth's atmosphere they burn up.

Meteor showers like the one in the picture happen when the Earth's orbit passes through some meteoroids.

As meteors burn up we see them on Earth as bright flashes of light.

a meteorite in South Africa

Some meteoroids are very big and do not burn up as they fall through the air to Earth. They fall to the surface of the Earth. They are called **meteorites**.

About 20,000 years ago a very large meteorite crashed into the ground. It left a hole about .6 miles across called the Meteor Crater where it landed in the Arizona desert.

New Worlds

How will people make use of space in the future? The picture shows machines being used to mine rocks from asteroids. Other machines carry the rocks back to a huge spacecraft.

Perhaps this will never happen but many dreams about space have now come true.

Glossary

asteroid belt   a part of space between Mars and Jupiter where there are thousands of asteroids.

asteroids   tiny planets, made out of lumpy rock, that orbit the Sun.

astronomer   someone who studies the stars, planets, and other objects in space.

atmosphere   the layer of gases that surround a planet or star.

axis   an imaginary straight line from the top to the bottom of a spinning object, such as the Earth. The object rotates or spins around this line.

binoculars   a kind of double telescope with two eyepieces.

canyon   a deep, narrow valley.

carbon dioxide   a gas without color or smell. It is found in the air on Earth and in the atmosphere of some other planets.

core   the center of something.

crater   a bowl-shaped hollow.

crescent   the shape of the young moon.

dune   a high bank of sand that is built up by the wind.

dust   tiny particles of solid matter.

earthquake   a sudden shaking of the land due to movements in the Earth's crust.

eclipse   the shadow caused by one object blocking off the light of another.

laser   an instrument that sends out a strong beam of light.

lava   hot, liquid rock that flows up from deep inside a planet.

lunar module   one of the three separate parts that make up a space rocket.

mantle   the layer of rock between the outer shell of a planet and its central part.

meteor   a piece of rock from space that burns up when it strikes the layer of gases around a planet. As it burns it makes a bright light in the sky.

meteorite   a piece of rock or metal from space that manages to pass through a planet's atmosphere without burning up.

meteoroid   a rock or metal that travels through space.

molten   metal or rock that has been melted by intense heat.

moons   smaller objects that travel around a planet. The planet Jupiter has 16 moons. The Earth has only one moon.

nitrogen   a gas found in the atmosphere of some planets. It has no color, taste, or smell, and does not burn.

north pole   the farthest point north on a planet.

orbit   a path through space made by one thing going around another. The Earth moves in orbit around the Sun.

oxygen   a gas found in air and water. Oxygen is important to all plants and animals. We cannot breathe without oxygen.

particles   tiny amounts of solid matter.

plain   a level, flat area of ground.

planet   an object in space that moves around a star like the Sun.

plate   a section of the Earth's outer crust.

radio telescope   a telescope that can pick up radio waves sent out from objects in space.

reflect   to throw back light from the surface of an object.

rocket   something that is made to move forward or upward very quickly. Rockets are used to lift spacecraft into space.

satellite   a small object in orbit around a larger object in space.

season   one of the four periods of time during the year.

Solar System   the Sun and all the objects that orbit it, such as the planets and their moons.

south pole   the farthest point south of the planet.

space probe   a machine sent from Earth to study objects in space. It does not have people on board.

Space Shuttle   an American space ship that can land again.

sulfuric acid   a liquid chemical that can destroy living things and eat through metal.

surface   the outside layer or top layer of something.

telescope   an instrument for looking at distant objects, or for picking up the rays that come from them.

volcano   a type of mountain that is formed when very hot liquid rock is forced up from deep inside a planet. The liquid cools leaving a mountain of rock.

water vapor   water in the form of a gas.

Index

Photographic credits *(t=top b=bottom l=left r=right)*
cover: to follow **title page:** Daily Telegraph Colour Library; 5 Science Photo Library; 6 Syndication International Limited; 8, 9, 11, 12, 16/17, 18, 19t Science Photo Library; 19b Frank Lane Picture Agency; 21 Science Photo Library; 22 ZEFA; 23t, 23b, 24, 25, 28, 30, 31, 32, 33, 34, 35, 37t Science Photo Library; 37b NASA; 39, 42t Science Photo Library; 42b John Mason; 43 Science Photo Library

Material used in this book first appeared in Macmillan World Library: *The Inner Planets.* Published by Heinemann Children's Reference.